D0578514

Fundamental
STRENGTH TRAINING

The following athletes were photographed for this book:
- Abdul Awad
- Marc Bell
- Bonne Chance
- Heather Clark
- Jeremy Cook
- Moriah Cooperson
- Cameron Darlington
- Nick Fonville
- James Goldsby
- Deidre Golej
- Koy Hardy
- Jaspreet Kalsi
- Chad Kim
- David Lee
- Myisha Love
- Mona Montoya
- Christina Muela
- Matt Peck
- Nate Sapington
- Kim Schwarzkopf
- Elizabeth Simas
- Brian Sims
- Sheri Sorensen
- Melissa Tews
- Fernando Trejo
- Janie Villegas
- Anne Williams

Fundamental
STRENGTH TRAINING

Jeff Savage

Photographs by Jimmy Clarke

Lerner Publications Company ● Minneapolis

Lerner Publications Company
A division of Lerner Publishing Group
241 First Avenue North
Minneapolis, MN 55401 U.S.A.

Website address: www.lernerbooks.com

The Fundamental Sports series was conceptualized by editor Julie Jensen, designed by graphic artist Michael Tacheny, and composed on a Macintosh computer by Robert Mauzy. The Fundamental Sports series was designed in conjunction with the Beginning Sports series to offer young athletes a basic understanding of various sports at two reading levels.

Photo Acknowledgments
Photos are reproduced with the permission of: Corbis-Bettmann, pp. 7, 8; UPI/Corbis-Bettmann, pp. 9 (top), 35 (top); Blank Archives/Archive Photos, p. 9 (bottom); Archive Photos, p. 10 (top); Gene Lester/Archive Photos, p. 10 (bottom); Stephen Downs/Archive Photos, p.11; © 1998/Nik Wheeler, p. 21; Reuters/Joe Giza/Archive Photos, p. 50; © ALLSPORT USA/Simon Bruty, p. 52; Reuters/Corbis-Bettmann, p. 55; SportsChrome East/West (David Lee Waite), p. 56 (left); © ALLSPORT USA/Bill Dobbins, p. 56 (right); © ALLSPORT USA/Doug Pensinger, p. 57 (both); © ALLSPORT USA/Rick Stewart, p. 58.
Artwork by Laura Westlund and John Erste.

Library of Congress Cataloging-in-Publication Data

Savage, Jeff, 1961–
    Fundamental strength training / Jeff Savage ; Jimmy Clarke, photographs.
        p. cm. — (Fundamental sports)
    Includes bibliographical references (p.) and index.
    Summary: An introduction to the sport of strength training, with and without weights, including its history, equipment, techniques, and variations.
    ISBN 0–8225-3461-4 (lib. bdg. : alk. paper)
    1. Weight lifting—Juvenile literature. 2. Bodybuilding—Juvenile literature. [1. Weight lifting. 2. Bodybuilding.] I. Clarke, Jimmy, ill. II. Series.
GV546.S28 1998
613.7'13—dc21   97–44292

Manufactured in the United States of America
2 3 4 5 6 7 – GPS – 06 05 04 03 02 01

Contents

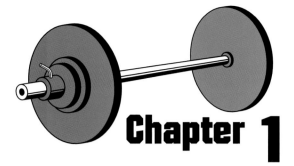

Chapter 1

How This Sport Got Started

Few people are natural athletes. Most of us have to work hard to excel at a sport. We are able to do only what our bodies will allow. One secret to success is improving our strength. Strength training—using weights, **resistance tools,** or simple exercises—increases strength and improves endurance. By doing exercises designed to increase strength, an athlete builds muscle tissue and increases the body's **metabolism.** Strength training therefore allows us to run faster, jump higher, throw a ball harder, and hit or kick a ball farther. In short, it improves our physical ability. Strength training does something else, too. It shapes our bodies and makes us feel better about ourselves.

Strength training is a safe form of exercise for most people, regardless of height, weight, or physical ability. It can be performed indoors or outdoors. It can be done alone or with other people. Strength training requires effort and dedication, and it teaches us patience.

7

Eugene Sandow

Eugene Sandow was a pioneer in American weight training. An Englishman who gained fame in the 1890s by performing great feats of strength, he first traveled across Europe as The Great Sandow, raising men over his head and even lifting horses into the air.

Sandow came to the United States at the turn of the century. He was promoted as the World's Strongest Man and became an instant celebrity. His routine was to step into a glass case, as though he were on display, and pose and flex his muscles in front of hundreds of admirers.

Sales of weight training equipment boomed. Thousands of men dreamed of becoming the next Sandow. Contests were held in which competitors compared muscles, and Sandow presented a golden statue of himself to the winners.

The History of Strength Training

The origin of strength training is unclear, but we do know that in ancient times men were honored for having muscular bodies. One early form of weight training in ancient Greece was stone lifting, in which men lifted heavy stones to increase their strength. That tradition evolved into the sport of weight lifting, in which people competed to see who could lift the most weight.

In the late 1800s, strength contests were held regularly in Europe. These were generally won by men with large, beefy bodies. The idea was "the bigger you are, the stronger you are." But such thinking changed in 1898 when George Hackenschmidt won the Russian weight lifting championship. Hackenschmidt, dubbed the Russian Lion, had a lean, wiry body with almost no fat. After winning the title, the Russian Lion emigrated to Great Britain and made a fortune demonstrating his feats of strength. He entertained audiences lifting four or more men off the ground with one arm and juggling 200-pound dumbbells while doing somersaults. Hackenschmidt was also a talented runner, jumper, swimmer, and wrestler—who competed for eight years and 2,000 bouts without losing a match.

Bernarr Macfadden and his daughters flex their muscles during a 1925 radio broadcast.

In 1903 Bernarr Macfadden, an American health enthusiast, sponsored a contest at Madison Square Garden in New York to select America's Most Perfectly Developed Man. The contestants were judged on muscle development rather than sheer strength, and the contest became a popular annual event. Angelo Siciliano, who won the contest in 1922, decided he could make a fortune with his muscular body. First he changed his name to Charles Atlas. Then he designed a muscle-development program based on **isotonic** resistance exercises that did not employ weights. He advertised the program—called Dynamic-Tension—in comic books and magazines. Millions of kids have seen the ad in which a skinny boy gets sand kicked in his face by a bully, takes the Charles Atlas course, and returns to the beach to beat up the bully.

In 1939 the first Mr. America contest, sponsored by the American Athletic Union, was held at Madison Square Garden. Other contests such as Mr. Universe and Mr. Olympia soon followed. **Bodybuilding** grew in popularity a decade later, when Steve Reeves won the Mr. America contest. Reeves lifted weights every day alongside the ocean in southern California at a place called Muscle Beach. His charm and muscular physique earned him fame and a career in the movies, including the title role in *Hercules*.

Top, Steve Reeves at left happily poses at Muscle Beach with his costars in the movie *Athena*. Above, a crowd gathers around a new weight-lifting machine at Muscle Beach in 1956.

Arnold Schwarzenegger

In 1967 Arnold Schwarzenegger won the Mr. Universe title and emigrated to the United States from Austria to gain fame, like Reeves, as a movie actor. Legions of young weight trainers idolize Schwarzenegger for his dedication to the sport and for his muscular build. While Schwarzenegger and others pursued weight training for the purpose of building up their bodies for contests based on physique, other athletes discovered that weight training could benefit them by increasing strength and improving performance in other sports.

As recently as the 1960s, however, weight training was considered bad for most athletes. Many people thought that adding muscle mass limited flexibility or range of motion. Vince Lombardi, coach of the Green Bay Packers, helped dispel that myth when his football players began an intense weight lifting program and then won the first two Super Bowls in 1967 and 1968. Soon all pro football players were lifting weights to match the strength of the Packers.

Women's competitions emerged in the 1970s, and bodybuilding stars like Cory Everson, Sandy Riddell, and five-time Ms. Olympia Lenda Murray gained fame. But most women in other sports still refrained from "bulking up."

It wasn't until the 1980s that athletes of finesse sports such as baseball, golf, and tennis realized the value of strength training. Even athletes in these non-collision sports found that strength training improved their batting, hitting, and speed. Rather than lose their touch as they feared, these athletes gained power and endurance.

Today most college and professional sports teams, for both men and women, have full-time strength and conditioning coaches. Health clubs are filled with weight training enthusiasts. Many high schools offer physical education courses involving weight lifting, and some junior high school programs are also joining in. Today more than one million people in the United States train with weights.

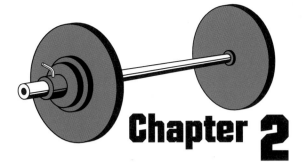

Chapter 2

BASICS

To train with weights, you will need the equipment and a suitable area in which to work out. Health clubs are everywhere, and most have trainers who can teach proper lifting techniques. Many schools have weight rooms where students can work out. Another option is to find a set of weights on sale at a sporting goods store or through the want-ads of a local newspaper.

The two types of weights are **free weights** and **weight machines.** Free weights consist of bars and plates made of iron. A simple set of free weights has a long bar called a barbell, two short bars called dumbbells, and at least 100 pounds of assorted weights. Machines are the devices usually found in health clubs. These modern contraptions are useful in exercising certain muscles, and they are fun to use.

13

A weight bench is an important piece of equipment. Many basic lifts are performed while sitting or lying on the bench. A weight bench is about the height and width of a picnic table bench but half as long. The bench you use should be padded for comfort and sturdy enough to support both you and the weight. Most weight benches are designed to also be raised at an angle, or incline. The bench then becomes an **incline bench.**

Certain lifts can only be performed on machines. But weight machines, which tend to work one or two muscle groups at a time, generally stimulate fewer muscle fibers per lift than free weights. The weight connected to machines typically slides along metal which helps guide the weight. Free weights, on the other hand, are not attached to anything. They must be balanced as well as lifted. This requires the use of more muscles. Free weights are more difficult to handle, especially for beginners. Yet for many exercises, they are the weight of choice of most serious lifters.

Free Weight Equipment

A weight room can contain a wide variety of equipment, and the type of equipment found in one weight room can differ greatly from that in another setting. After you familiarize yourself with the benches, barbells, dumbbells, pulleys, and other devices available in your weight room, you may still feel lost in a different setting. Never be afraid to ask questions if you don't know how to use a piece of equipment. Most high school and health club weight rooms have professional staff members who can assist you. If help is unavailable, stick to the basics—situps, pushups, chinups, and exercises using a regular bench, dumbbells, a barbell.

Clothing is important in weight training. You should wear comfortable, loose-fitting clothes such as shorts and a T-shirt. Athletic shoes are important for solid footing. It is unwise to lift weights barefooted or in dress shoes.

Getting Ready

Be sure to warm up and stretch before training with weights. Some beginners skip warmups and stretches and go straight to the weights. Such eagerness can result in injury. Always take a few minutes to warm up and stretch.

Many weight lifters wear gloves while training to protect their hands. Gloves are not essential but they do provide comfort.

Some weight lifters wear a heavy belt around their waist to support their lower back muscles. But a belt is not necessary unless you are lifting more than your own body weight.

Christina warms up on a stair-climbing machine.

The purpose of warming up is to get oxygen carried by your blood to your muscles. Remember, your muscles need oxygen to breathe, too. One way to warm up your muscles is to run for a couple of minutes. You can run around a track or on a treadmill like Christina and Moriah. Anne rides for 10 minutes on a stationary bike. Chad jumps rope for awhile for a warmup.

Another good way to warm up is to lift very light weight. You could lift the dumbbell bars (without weights) a dozen times or so in several different motions described in the next chapter. Or if you are stronger, you can use the barbell (it weighs 45 pounds).

Ready for the weights? Not so fast. Now that you have warmed up, you need to stretch your muscles. And as important as it is to stretch before strength training, it is just as important to stretch afterward. When stretching your muscles, hold every stretch without bouncing. Bouncing can cause injury. When stretching leg muscles, be sure to keep from locking your knees, which can also cause injury. Here are a few easy stretching exercises to perform before and after your workout.

Shoulder shrugs loosen the upper back and shoulders. Marc stands upright with his feet shoulder width apart. He raises both shoulders up toward his neck, as if shrugging, then lowers them. Marc repeats this movement 10 times.

Triceps stretches loosen the muscles at the back side of the upper arm. David raises his left arm and grasps his left elbow with his right hand. He pulls gently to the right until he feels the muscle stretching and holds it for 10 seconds. David repeats with the opposite arm.

Side bends stretch the sides of your body. Heather, Mona, Jaspreet, and Janie stand with their feet shoulder width apart. Along with the others, Heather raises her right arm over her head and bends slowly to the left, with her left arm sliding down her side. She holds this position for 20 seconds, then repeats it on the opposite side.

Sky stretches are similar to side bends, except they stretch the upper back as well. Perform them as you would side bends, but aim the reaching hand toward the sky.

Forward bends (also called hamstring stretches) stretch the back of your legs and your lower back. Stand upright with your feet together. Bend forward and reach toward your feet. Keep your knees slightly bent, holding this position for at least 30 seconds.

Quadriceps stretches stretch the muscles at the front of your thighs. Kim stands with her feet shoulder-width apart. She reaches behind her back and grips her right ankle with her right hand, pulling her foot toward her buttocks. Kim holds this position for at least 30 seconds and then repeats with the opposite side.

Calf stretches are for the back of your lower legs. Kim puts one foot in front of the other and places both hands against a wall. Leaning forward, she keeps the heel of her back foot on the floor until she feels her calf stretch. She holds this position for 20 seconds and then repeats with the opposite leg. If you have a partner to stretch with, lean against each other's shoulders.

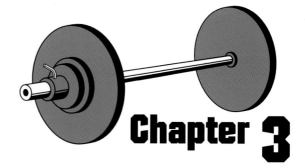

Chapter 3

THE LIFTS

Strength training can be performed without weights. Many exercises, commonly known as **calisthenics,** can be performed wherever you have enough room to do them. Pushups build chest muscles. Chinups build upper back muscles. Dips develop arm and chest muscles. Squats build leg muscles. Situps build stomach muscles. You will get a thorough workout and make great gains in strength by performing these exercises on a regular basis.

To do a wider variety of exercises, strength trainers depend on resistance equipment, free weights, and weight machines. Resistance exercises can be performed with a partner creating pressure or with resistance equipment, such as a piece of rubber tubing. When

Muscles

The human body has more than 600 muscles. Each muscle is composed of bundles of fiber. When you lift a weight you exercise a portion of the fiber. The heavier the weight, or the more times you lift it, the more fiber you exercise.

When muscle fibers are exercised, they actually break down. Muscles respond to the exertion by repairing broken down fibers and building them up bigger and stronger than they were.

strength training, always remember the basic rules. Quit or do fewer reps than planned if you can't continue without cheating. Exhale when lifting, or exerting the most effort, and inhale when returning to the starting position. This rule also applies to exercises that don't use weights. For example, when doing situps, exhale while raising your head and shoulders off the floor, and inhale on the way back down.

The main thing to keep in mind as you weight train is this—weights are heavy! If you hold the plates the wrong way, you might end up with a smashed toe. If you load the plates onto the barbell the wrong way, you could wind up with an injured back. There are two simple safety rules to follow. One, always use both hands when holding plates. Two, always bend your knees when lifting plates from the floor and loading them onto the bar. (And once you've slipped the plates onto the bar, be sure to fasten the collars with their locking screws.) Weights must be handled with care. Once you understand this, you are ready to perform some basic lifts.

The six main body regions that are exercised are the chest, back, shoulders, arms, abdomen, and legs. There are several basic lifts for each of these areas of the body. You can incorporate the following exercises into a weekly program similar to the one outlined in chapter 4.

Human Muscular System

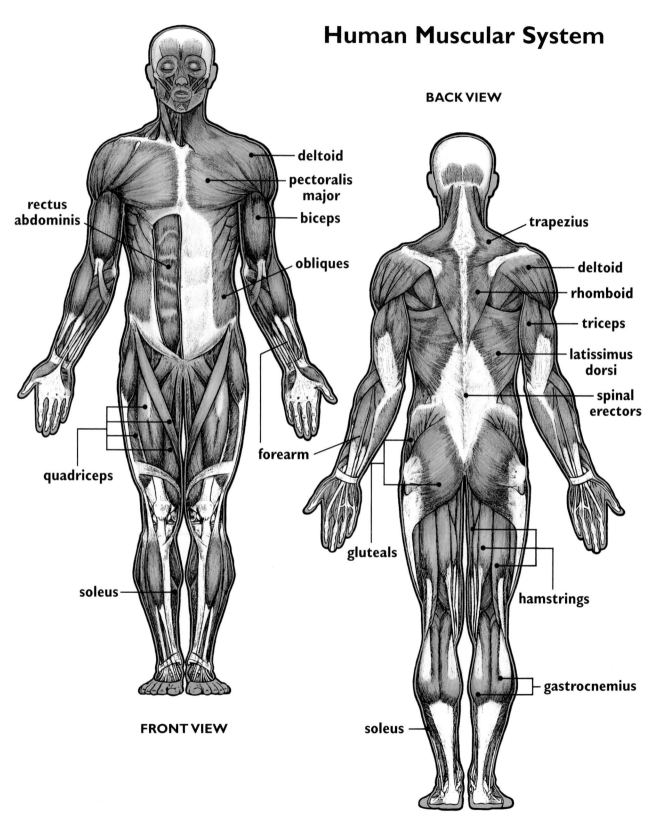

BACK VIEW

deltoid

pectoralis
major

biceps

rectus
abdominis

obliques

trapezius

deltoid

rhomboid

triceps

latissimus
dorsi

spinal
erectors

quadriceps

forearm

gluteals

hamstrings

soleus

gastrocnemius

soleus

FRONT VIEW

Chest

The main chest muscles are called pectorals (pecs for short). Pectorals are the main muscles used in pushing and punching.

● *Bench Press*

Bench presses are a common lift to develop the pectoral muscles. Brian lies on the bench on his back with his feet firmly on the floor for balance. He grips the bar with both hands, positioned about a foot wider than shoulder width apart. (A narrower grip would work more on triceps muscles.) He lifts the bar off the rack and supports it at arm's length. Then Brian lowers the bar slowly toward his chest, keeping his elbows out to the sides. He touches the bar gently to his chest and comes to a split-second stop. He then presses the bar upward until his arms are extended, stopping just short of locking his elbows. That completes one **repetition, or rep.**

Moriah completes some reps on a bench press machine.

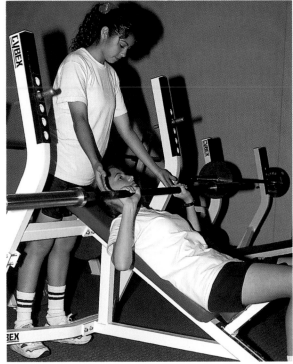

● *Incline Bench Press*

Incline bench presses are important for developing the upper pectorals. Moriah lies back on the incline bench with her feet on the floor. She grips the bar as she would for a regular bench press, lifting the bar off the rack and holding it straight up. Moriah then lowers the bar slowly toward her upper chest. She touches the bar gently to her chest, stopping for a moment, then presses it back up to the starting position. Like Moriah, be careful to balance the bar in this exercise.

Bench presses and incline bench presses can be performed using dumbbells as well. James holds the dumbbells with his palms facing forward and executes the presses the same way as barbell presses are done.

● Fly

Flys, another type of chest lift, also help develop the pectoral muscles. Nick lies on the bench as he would for presses. He holds a dumbbell in each hand, palms facing each other, directly above his chest. Nick lowers the dumbbells out and down to either side in a wide arc, stopping when the weights reach below shoulder level. He is careful to keep his elbows bent slightly and the weight under control. Slowly lifting the weight back upward through the arc, as if giving someone a big bear hug, Nick returns the dumbbells to the starting position.

Flys can be performed on machines as well. Fly machines are sometimes known as "pec decks" and are useful for making already developed muscles more defined. Moriah keeps her feet on the floor and her back against the back rest when executing machine flys.

Back

The muscles of the back include the trapezius, latissimus dorsi, rhomboids, and spinal erectors. The trapezius (traps) is a triangular muscle that extends from the neck to the shoulder blades. The latissimus dorsi (lats) are the large triangular muscles that extend from the shoulders to the lower back. They are the largest muscles of the upper body, functioning to pull the arms back. The rhomboids are smaller muscles between the traps and lats. The spinal erectors are a set of muscles in the lower back that keep the spine erect.

● *Traps*

Dumbbell shrugs and upright rows are two main lifts to develop the traps.

Marc demonstrates dumbbell shrugs. He stands upright with a dumbbell in each hand at his sides. Keeping his arms straight, Marc raises his shoulders up as high as he can until he feels a squeeze. He holds it for a moment, then returns to the starting position. He tries not to move anything but his shoulders in this exercise.

Upright rows are performed with the barbell. Standing with her feet at shoulder width and her knees bent slightly, Kim holds the bar out in front with an overhand grip and hands about a foot apart. She lifts the bar to her chin, holds it for a split-second, then lowers it to the starting position. She is careful not to sway or bend her back.

● *Lats*

Chinups develop mainly the lat muscles. (Chinups also strengthen biceps muscles, which are discussed later.) Kim grabs the chinning bar with an underhand grip with her hands positioned about a foot wider than shoulder width apart. She hangs from the bar, then pulls herself up until her chin reaches the bar. She holds that position for a moment, then lowers herself to the starting position. Reverse chinups are done the same way except you pull yourself up with an overhand grip, touching the chinning bar with the back of the neck.

To do a chinup you must lift your entire body weight. If you are unable to do this, a lat machine is useful. A lat machine allows you to duplicate the movement of chinups while lifting a lighter weight. Use a long bar and grasp it with a wide overhand grip. Sit on the seat with your knees locked under the support bar. Pull the bar down to the back of your neck, hold it for a moment, then allow the bar to raise back up.

● *Lower Back*

Rows are great for developing the lower back muscles. One-arm dumbbell rows are performed with one dumbbell and the bench. Melissa positions herself with her right knee and right hand on the bench and bends forward so her upper body is parallel to the floor. She holds the dumbbell in her left hand with her arm extended to the floor. Melissa pulls the dumbbell upward to her side, keeping her body steady. Pausing at the top, she then lowers the dumbbell back toward the floor.

Seated cable rows are performed on a machine. Moriah and Anne sit with their feet braced against the crossbar and their knees bent slightly. They grab the handles and pull them in toward the lower chest. Sitting upright, Moriah pushes her chest out to meet the handles. She pauses for a moment, then lets the handles go forward to the starting position.

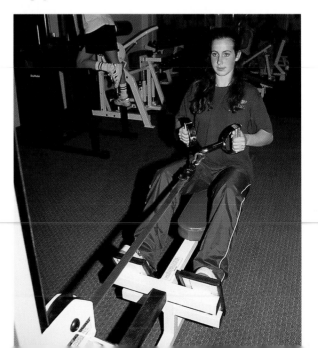

Shoulders

The main shoulder muscles are called deltoids. Each arm supports three deltoids—the anterior (front), medial (middle), and posterior (rear). The deltoids help raise the upper arm. Other muscles deep inside the shoulder help rotate the joint.

● *Front Deltoids*

Military presses and Arnolds develop the front deltoids. To perform military presses, Myisha sits on the bench with her feet on the floor. She holds the bar with a wide overhand grip in front of her chest. Myisha lifts the bar straight over her head until her arms are extended, stopping just short of locking her elbows. She then lowers the weight back to the starting position.

Spotter

A spotter is a person who stands near you as you perform your exercises. The spotter makes sure you are using good form by helping guide the movement of the weights. The spotter is ready to help you if the weight begins to slip from your grip or becomes too heavy for you to lift. The spotter encourages you to complete sets and pushes you to train hard. The spotter is a valuable part of your workout.

Arnolds are named for the famous weight trainer Arnold Schwarzenegger, who invented them. Starting either standing or seated, hold two dumbbells at shoulder height with palms toward you. Koy lifts the dumbbells straight up over her head while turning them so that they face out at the top of the lift. She reverses the movement as she lowers the weights to the starting position.

● *Middle Deltoids*

The middle deltoids can be exercised by performing behind-the-head presses. Kim sits on the bench with her feet on the floor, holding the bar behind her head with a wide overhand grip. Keeping her elbows pressed as far back as possible, Kim lifts the bar straight up over her head. She then carefully lowers the weight to the starting position. She does not rest the bar on her neck, because that could cause serious injury.

● *Rear Deltoids*

Lateral raises develop the rear deltoids. Sheri, Jaspreet, and Janie stand with their feet shoulder width apart and knees bent slightly. With a dumbbell in each hand, they bend forward slightly and lift the weights up and out to the side, with the palms facing the floor. They raise the dumbbells slightly higher than shoulder height, then lower them slowly back to the starting position.

Arms

The muscles of the arms include the biceps, triceps, and forearm. The biceps is the muscle at the front of the arm above the elbow that is often flexed to indicate strength. The triceps is the muscle at the back of the arm above the elbow. The triceps acts to straighten the arm at the elbow. The forearm group of muscles encircles the arm between the elbow and wrist. These muscles work to move the hand up and down.

● Biceps

Curls develop the biceps. Standing barbell curls are the most popular biceps exercise. Standing up straight with his feet a few inches apart and knees bent slightly, Fernando holds the bar with an underhand grip, hands shoulder width apart. He pulls the bar up and in a wide arc toward his neck. He slowly lowers the weight to the starting position.

Handicapped Lifters

Many different people with handicaps or disabilities do strength training exercises and benefit from them the same as everyone else. Specially challenged kids can do situps, pushups, chinups, and exercises with resistance tools. They also can do all the lifts—presses, squats, lunges, flys, curls. Having a spotter present to offer guidance and support makes lifting fun and safe for kids with handicaps as well as younger kids or people with no weight training experience.

Arnold Schwarzenegger coaches a Special Olympics weight training program.

Alternate dumbbell curls can be performed either standing or sitting. Jeremy holds a dumbbell in each hand at his sides, with his palms facing inward. He curls his right hand out and up to the right shoulder, turning his palm toward the shoulder. He keeps his elbow close to his side through the movement. Jeremy lowers his right hand at the same time he curls his left hand up to the left shoulder. Then he lowers his left hand as he curls his right arm, continuously alternating arms.

● *Triceps*

Triceps are strengthened with extensions and cable pressdowns. To perform extensions, lie on the bench on your back with knees bent and feet flat on the bench. Holding the barbell in an overhand grip, with his hands about 10 inches apart, Fernando presses the barbell up over his head until his arms are extended. He does not lock his elbows. Slowly lowering the barbell to just above his forehead, Fernando remembers to keep his elbows in.

You can also perform extensions with a single dumbbell. Seated with the dumbbell behind your head, raise your arm straight up. Do not lock your elbow. Carefully lower the dumbbell back behind your head. Alternate arms.

To perform cable pressdowns, you will need to use a piece of equipment found in most weight rooms—a **pulley**. Standing with her feet shoulder width apart and knees bent, Deidre holds a short bar hooked to a pulley with both hands in an overhand grip. The weights are attached to the other end of the pulley. Deidre presses the bar down in front of her body until her arms straighten, without locking her elbows. She lets the bar come back up until her arms are parallel to the floor, keeping her elbows in.

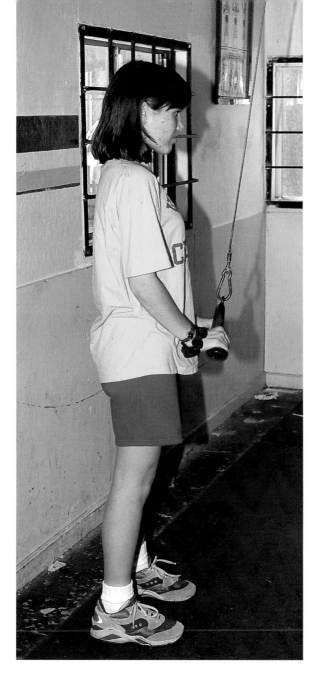

Forearms can be developed with wrist curls. Kim sits on the bench, holding a dumbbell with an overhand grip and resting her forearms on her thighs. She turns her wrists in a forward motion, lowering the weight slightly. Then she bends her wrists the opposite way to raise the weight back up. The dumbbell only moves a few inches in each direction.

Abdomen

The main muscles of the abdomen are the rectus abdominis and the external obliques. The abdominis muscles (abs) extend from the lower chest to just below your stomach. They pull the torso toward the lower body. The obliques extend along each side of the torso. Their function is to bend, rotate, and turn the torso.

● Abs

Situps develop your upper abs, and leg raises build your lower abs. For regular situps, Kim lies on her back on the floor, clasping her hands behind her neck. She bends her knees and keeps her feet flat on the floor. You may tuck your feet under a support, such as an armchair, or have a partner hold them down. In a short, contracted movement, Kim slowly raises her upper torso a few inches off the floor. She pauses, then slowly returns to the floor. Do not sit up all the way to your knees, and do not jerk your body up.

Incline board situps are performed in much the same way but on a board, with the head lower than the feet—a position that makes the exercise more difficult. Lie on the incline board with your feet locked under a padded bar. Fold your arms in an X across your chest and lift your upper torso off the board, then lower back down carefully.

Twisting situps are a variation of regular situps. Kim twists slightly to one side as she nears the top of the situp, pointing one elbow at the opposite knee and then alternating. Again, she does not raise up more than a few inches and does not jerk up quickly.

Regular leg raises are best performed on a mat. Kim lies on her back with her hands facing palms down at her sides. She slowly raises her legs straight up without bending at the knees. Kim holds her legs for a moment about two feet from the ground, then slowly lowers them to the mat.

Bent-knee leg raises are performed on an incline board. Lie on your back on the board with your head higher than your feet. Grab the board behind your head, bend your knees, and raise your legs as high as you can. Exhale as you raise. Slowly lower your legs back to the board while inhaling.

● *Obliques*

Obliques can be exercised with side leg raises. Kim lies on her side on the floor with her elbow tucked under her for support. She bends her lower leg and keeps her upper leg straight. Kim raises her upper leg as high as she can, then lowers it again. She doesn't use her hips.

Crunches are great for developing the entire abdomen. Abdul and James lie on their backs on the floor, with their hands clasped behind the head and knees bent. They lift their head and shoulders toward the knees while at the same time pulling the knees in toward the shoulders. Like Abdul and James, you should feel your stomach muscles "crunch."

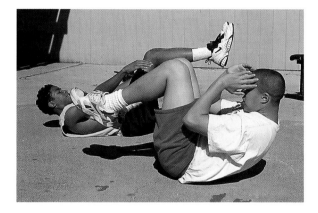

Legs

The main leg muscles are the quadriceps, gluteals, hamstring, soleus, and gastrocnemius. The quadriceps (quads) are a group of four muscles that form the front of the thigh. The quads extend the lower leg at the knee, such as in kicking. The gluteals (glutes) form the rear end. The glutes work to push the upper leg backward and to spread the legs apart. The hamstring is the muscle group at the back of the thigh. These muscles work when bending the leg up toward the hip. The soleus and gastrocnemius muscles form the calf. The calf muscles provide power and spring when jumping, running, and pushing with the legs.

Squats, lunges, and leg presses are good overall leg exercises that focus on the quads and glutes. To perform squats, Abdul stands with his feet shoulder width apart and toes turned slightly out. He balances a barbell across the back of his shoulders. Keeping his head up and back straight, Abdul slowly bends at the knees and lowers to the ground in a squat position. Then he pushes himself back up to the starting position.

Lunges are similar to squats, except you take a step forward as you lower the weight. Your trailing knee should almost touch the floor. For beginners, dumbbells are easier to use for lunges. Simply hold the dumbbells at your sides as you step.

Leg presses are performed on a machine. Jeremy sits on the machine with his knees bent and his feet side by side on the platform. He pushes down, raising his body and the weight, straightening his legs but not locking his knees. Then he bends at the knees, lowering the weight.

Leg curls develop the back thighs. Anne lies face down on the leg curl machine and places her heels under the curl bar. She pulls the bar up and in toward her body as far as she can. Slowly Anne then lowers it back to the starting position.

Standing calf raises develop the calves. A stationary platform of some kind, about four inches high, is all that is needed for this exercise. Matt stands with his feet shoulder width apart on a block of wood. He balances a barbell across the upper shoulders. With his knees bent slightly, Matt lowers his heels as far as he can toward the floor. Then he raises back up as high as possible until he is on his toes.

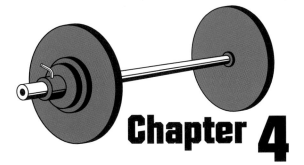

Chapter 4

WORKOUT

Once you have learned how to perform some basic lifts, you will want to put your knowledge to use. But what lifts should you do? How often should you do them? How much weight do you use? To get the most out of your workout, you need to know a few terms first.

To develop your muscles, a certain amount of weight must be lifted a number of times. Each time a weight is lifted, it is called a repetition (rep). A series of repetitions (usually between 8 and 12) is called a **set.** A group of 1 to 5 sets is recommended for young athletes. A series of different lifts and exercises is called a **workout routine.** A sequence of workout routines is called a **program.**

Beginning lifters should use enough weight to perform at least 8 reps but no more than 12. When doing a set, more muscle fiber is activated after the second rep, more after the third, and so on, until all the muscle's fiber is working by about the eighth rep. If you cannot do 8 reps with the amount of weight you've selected, use less weight for your next set. If you can do more than 12 reps, add more weight for your next set. Doing the last few reps of each set should be difficult. If not, use more weight. Be sure to rest for at least one minute between sets. This is the amount of time necessary for blood to flush through the muscle, removing metabolic waste (which is created as the muscle is worked) and replenishing energy.

Anne works out on the leg extension machine.

The amount of weight you lift depends on what you are trying to achieve. Lifters who desire increased strength and bigger muscles should lift more weight and do fewer reps. Athletes who want to focus on endurance and muscle toning should lift less weight and do more reps. Whether you fit either of these descriptions or fall somewhere in between, an important part of anyone's workout is warming up and stretching before lifting.

Once you have completed your workout for the day, your muscles must be given a chance to rest. Muscles need time to recover and grow. Working the same muscles day after day will not make them grow faster, and likely will tear them down and slow their growth. As a rule, it is best not to exercise the same muscles two days in a row. What's more, the muscles actually grow while at rest. So as your chest muscles rest on their day off, that is when they are growing.

Following is a simple training program that involves working out three days a week. You can design your own workout program in whatever way best suits your schedule and the availability of equipment, but be sure you give your muscles at least a day of rest between workouts. Some trainers believe that lifters ideally should work out a minimum of three days a week, so that no more than three days go by between workouts.

Nutrition

Proper nutrition is always important, but it is essential when weight training. Strenuous exercise takes energy, which comes from a single source—food. Without the right food in your body, you will not have the energy to exercise.

You've probably heard the phrase "well-balanced diet." This is what you need to eat to perform in the weight room. What exactly is meant by well-balanced? It means a proper mix of proteins, carbohydrates, fats, minerals, vitamins, and water.

Protein comes mainly from fish, chicken and other meats, eggs, and beans. The body uses protein to create muscle tissue. Without enough protein, muscles will not grow.

Carbohydrates come mostly from potatoes, pasta, tortillas, rice, and other grains, vegetables, and fruits. Carbohydrates provide the energy needed to exercise.

Fats are found in many foods and are important in small quantities. Fat supplies the body with a cushion to protect the heart and other organs. But too much fat is unhealthy. Food energy is measured in calories, and the amount of fat eaten each day should not, as a general rule, be more than 20 percent of total calories consumed.

A common myth in weight training is the more you eat, the more your muscles will grow. One professional bodybuilder eats 48 eggs a day, thinking the more protein he consumes, the bigger his muscles will grow. That's crazy. The truth is, if you eat a lot of food, most of it will be stored as fat. For instance, a 150-pound body can only process 23 grams of protein (about 3 egg whites) every 2 hours. The rest will turn directly to fat. The correct rule is this—eat a well-balanced diet and train hard, and you will see your body grow stronger.

Bench presses

MONDAY

Chest

bench barbell presses	4 sets
bench dumbbell presses	3 sets
incline bench barbell presses	4 sets
incline bench dumbbell presses	3 sets
flys	4 sets

Triceps

extensions	4 sets
cable pressdowns	4 sets

Abdomen

situps	30 reps
incline board situps	20 reps

WEDNESDAY

Back

dumbbell shrugs	4 sets
upright barbell rows	3 sets
chinups (or lats)	4 sets
one-arm dumbbell rows (or seated cable rows)	4 sets

Biceps

standing barbell curls	4 sets
alternate dumbbell curls	3 sets
wrist curls	3 sets

Abdomen

twisting situps	25 reps
bent-knee leg raises	25 reps

FRIDAY

Shoulders

military presses	4 sets
Arnolds	3 sets
behind-the-back presses	4 sets
lateral raises	3 sets

Legs

squats (or lunges)	4 sets
leg presses	4 sets
leg curls	4 sets
standing calf raises	3 sets

Abdomen

side leg raises	30 reps
crunches	35 reps

Leg curls

Standing barbell curls

Training Right

Remember, when you are doing any of these exercises, to perform them correctly. Many lifters, especially beginners, try to lift more weight than they can handle. They'll see their friends bench pressing 180 pounds, for example, and they'll try to lift just as much. This can cause lots of problems without doing anything to improve strength. Perfect form and technique are vital in strength training. Cheating to lift more weight or to do more repetitions, like swaying your back to do a few more arm curls, can cause serious injury. If you cheat on a lift, you are not exercising the intended muscle and, worse yet, you are risking a problem that could keep you from continuing your strength training. Never be embarrassed about the amount of weight you can lift. The point is, you are training and you are improving. And if you perform the lifts with good form and technique, you will get stronger.

Jose Canseco

Slugger Jose Canseco credits his great success in baseball to weight training. Jose was not picked until the 15th round of the baseball draft in 1982 by the Oakland A's. He wasn't expected to do much, and for a few years in the minors he didn't.

Then Jose began lifting weights. A's strength coach Dave McKay put Jose on a weight training program to build his upper body. By 1986 Jose was bigger, stronger, and faster. He made the A's major league team and belted 33 homers to win Rookie of the Year honors.

By 1988 Jose had packed on 40 pounds of muscle. That year he became the first player in history to hit 40 home runs and steal 40 bases in the same season. He was the unanimous choice as baseball's Most Valuable Player.

Jose spends two hours a day in the weight room. He concentrates on performing each lift correctly. Coach McKay says, "Jose will never cheat on a lift. He will do it with perfect form and technique."

Jose's twin brother, Ozzie, is also a baseball player. But Ozzie has not been a dedicated weight lifter like Jose, and he has spent most of his career in the minor leagues. Meanwhile, Jose continues pounding homers and stealing bases in the majors.

Not long ago, many coaches of various sports urged athletes to avoid weight training. They feared that lifting weights made athletes overly bulky, less agile, and slower. That notion has since been disproved. Athletes can make great gains in strength without losing a bit of flexibility or speed. When competitors of equal skill are matched in physical contests, the stronger one usually triumphs. For this reason, it is rare today to find a professional athlete who does not do some form of strength training.

The types of lifts athletes perform depend on the muscles they use most in their sport. Downhill skier Picabo Street, for instance, does a lot of lifts for her legs. Football linebacker Junior Seau is constantly improving his upper body strength. Swimmer Janet Evans lifts weights to strengthen her arms. These athletes understand the value of weight training.

Sports and the lifts that help you do your best at each one:

	Baseball	Basketball	Biking	Football	Golf	Gymnastics	Hockey	Soccer	Softball	Skiing	Swimming	Tennis	Track and Field	Volleyball	Wrestling
bench presses	X		X	X			X	X	X				X	X	X
flys			X			X					X			X	
shrugs				X		X									X
upright rows			X	X		X				X	X		X		X
chinups		X	X	X		X				X	X		X		X
rows			X									X			
military presses		X		X				X							X
Arnolds		X		X							X				X
lateral raises		X			X	X						X			
cable pressdowns	X	X							X		X	X		X	X
wrist curls	X		X		X		X		X			X		X	
abdominal exercises						X		X			X	X	X	X	X
squats	X	X	X	X	X	X	X	X	X	X					X
lunges	X			X	X		X	X	X	X					X
leg presses				X		X		X		X	X		X	X	
leg curls							X	X		X		X	X		
standing calf raises		X		X		X	X	X			X		X	X	

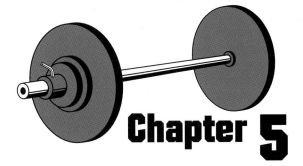

Chapter 5

COMPETITION

Strength training is mainly a competition with yourself, to help you improve your body's fitness, power, and endurance. Competing against others at a young age is not a good idea, because growing bodies are more prone to injury under stress. In addition, overtraining can cause problems such as loss of body weight, chronic soreness, and increase in illness. There are, however, some experienced professional and amateur lifters who do compete against others.

There are three groups of professional weight lifters. They are **Olympic lifters, power lifters,** and bodybuilders. Anyone can be a professional weight lifter, but becoming a champion takes years of patience and dedication.

Steroids

Steroids are a group of synthetic chemical compounds that affect growth and development of tissues, the reproductive cycle, and behavior. Some professional bodybuilders take steroids (orally or by injection) to enhance their physique when they have reached their muscle peak or "plateaued." Though most bodybuilding competitions still do not test for steroids, taking them is cheating.

Beginning and intermediate weight lifters believe they can increase muscle mass by taking steroids. This is false. Steroids do not necessarily build bigger muscles. And the slight effect the drugs do have on fully developed muscles lasts only a short time.

Steroids can cause serious and permanent damage to your body. Abuse of steroids leads to aggression, headaches, nosebleeds, dizziness, acne, hair loss, high blood pressure, blood clots, liver cancer, and death. Steroids are illegal drugs and they are dangerous.

53

Power lifting

Power lifting competitions involve three lifts—the bench press, the squat, and the dead lift. The bench press and the squat are lifts we have already discussed. The third lift, the dead lift, is performed simply by lifting the barbell from the floor to a standing position. The lifter uses mostly his thigh and back muscles by crouching down, grabbing the bar with an alternate grip (one palm facing outward, the other inward), and standing up with it. In all three lifts, the weight must be moving upward in a steady fashion. If the weight stops moving, even for an instant, a red light flashes and the lift is declared unsuccessful.

Power lifters compete year round in tournaments around the world. There are several weight classes (in which lifters are grouped according to weight) to make the competition fair. The competitor of each weight class who lifts the most weight combined in all three lifts is declared the winner.

Bodybuilding

Like power lifters, bodybuilders compete in tournaments, such as Mr. America and Mr. Universe. Unlike power lifters, bodybuilders do not lift weight during the competition. They are judged on how well their muscles are developed. They stand on a stage and flex their muscles for the judges. Posing is very important.

Achim Albrecht, winner of the Mr. Universe title in 1990, poses with his medal.

Bodybuilders spend most of the year lifting heavy weights to gain as much muscle mass as possible. They also follow a strict diet plan to achieve low body fat. While they are training, bodybuilders do not look like they do in magazines or on stage. They pace their workouts so that they peak at the right time for competitions.

Lenda Murray wins the Ms. Olympia title.

Many women compete in bodybuilding contests.

Because bodybuilders must keep very aware of every bite of food they take, they become nutrition experts as well as weight lifters. Several weeks before a competition, bodybuilders alter their diets to trim excess body fat. Less body fat makes muscles look more defined or "ripped." It takes many years of hard work to excel at bodybuilding competitions.

Olympic lifting

Olympic lifting involves two lifts—the clean and jerk and the snatch. The barbell is used for both lifts. The clean and jerk is a two-movement lift. The first part is performed by taking the barbell from the floor and lifting it to the chest. The lifter assumes a deep squatting position, holds the barbell with an overhand grip, and then pulls the bar upward (similar to the movement in an upright row), and stands straight up. The second part of the movement is performed by lifting the barbell over the head. The lifter jumps and spreads his legs to help in this movement.

The snatch is performed by taking the barbell from the floor to overhead in one movement. The lifter uses a wide overhand grip, bends at the knees, lifts the bar to waist level, squats low beneath it, and stands up—all in one motion. Both lifts require quickness and good technique. Unlike power lifting, Olympic lifting does not rely on strength alone.

Olympic lifters compete in tournaments each year, including the world championships, with the hope of qualifying for the ultimate meet held every four years—the summer Olympic Games. Olympic lifting has been a part of the Games since the original modern Olympic Games were held in 1896 in Athens, Greece. At the 1996 summer Olympics in Atlanta, 240 athletes

Pablo Lara of Cuba, performing the snatch lift, won a gold medal at the 1996 Olympic Games.

from over 80 countries competed in weight lifting.

The first round of Olympic lifting competition is held the first 10 days of the Games. There are 10 weight classes—ranging from 54 kilograms to 108 kilograms-and-over (119 pounds to 238 pounds-and-over), with one weight class competing each day. The top finishers in each class advance to the final round, which is held the final two days of the Games. One competitor from each class wins, based on the combined weights of the two lifts.

In both rounds of competition, each competitor gets three chances to lift as much weight as possible in the clean and jerk. Then the competitors get three chances at the snatch. The highest weights for each of the two lifts is combined to give that person's total weight. A competitor who fails at all three attempts in either of the lifts scores a zero for that lift.

Women's weight lifting made its debut at the 2000 Olympic Games in Sydney, Australia. Strong women from all over the world competed in the clean and jerk and snatch events.

Tara Nott

Tara Nott was a former gymnast and soccer player before she became interested in weight lifting in 1995. In very little time, she revealed a natural talent for the sport, earning her first of four national titles in 1996.

During the 2000 U.S. Weight Lifting National Championships, Nott and fellow weight lifter, Robin Goad, competed as each lifted a total of 177.5 kilograms (391.25 pounds). However, because Nott weighed .02 kilograms less than Goad, Nott was awarded first place.

At the 2000 Olympic trials, Nott hit all six of her lifts and broke all three records in the 48-kilogram (106-pound) division. Her performance earned Nott a spot in the 2000 Olympic Games in Sydney.

In Sydney, Nott lifted a total of 185 kilograms (407 pounds) in the women's 48-kilogram/106-pound competition and was awarded the silver medal. However, because drug tests showed that gold medallist Izabela Dragneva of Bulgaria had been under the influence of a banned substance while competing, the gold medal was awarded to Tara Nott.

60

Power lifting World Records

SQUAT	Weight Lifted	Name	Body Weight	Nationality	Date of Lift
Men	1,003 lbs.	Kirk Karwoski	276 lbs.	USA	7-23-97
	837 lbs.	Mike Bridges	182 lbs.	USA	7-10-82
	612 lbs.	Andrzej Stanaszek	115 lbs.	Poland	8-10-97
Junior Men	987 lbs.	Shane Hamman	276+ lbs.	USA	7-31-94
	757 lbs.	Pat Roche	182 lbs.	USA	7-27-91
	573 lbs.	Chun-Hsiung Hu	123 lbs.	TPE	8-10-97
Women	612 lbs.	Juanita Trujillo	198+ lbs.	USA	7-31-94
	540 lbs.	Anne Sigrid Stiklestad	165 lbs.	Norway	6-20-97
	377 lbs.	Raija Koskinen	106 lbs.	Finland	8-9-97
Junior Women	584 lbs.	Chia-Sui Lee	198+ lbs.	TPE	8-9-97
	474 lbs.	Valida Iskandarova	149 lbs.	Kazakhstan	6-20-97
	336 lbs.	Svetlana Tesleva	97 lbs.	Russia	12-6-96

BENCH PRESS	Weight Lifted	Name	Body Weight	Nationality	Date of Lift
Men	711 lbs.	James Henderson	276+ lbs.	USA	7-13-97
	442 lbs.	Alexei Sivokon	149 lbs.	Kazakhstan	8-10-97
	413 lbs.	Magnus Carlsson	123 lbs.	Sweden	11-14-96
Junior Men	557 lbs.	Daisuke Midote	276 lbs.	Japan	7-9-95
	474 lbs.	Jan Germanus	182 lbs.	SLK	6-24-94
	391 lbs.	Andrzej Stanaszek	115 lbs.	Poland	11-16-94
Women	386 lbs.	Chen-Yeh Chao	198+ lbs.	TPE	8-9-97
	259 lbs.	Carrie Boudreau	123 lbs.	USA	8-9-97
	187 lbs.	Svetlana Tesleva	97 lbs.	Russia	12-6-96
Junior Women	342 lbs.	Natalia Payusova	198 lbs.	Russia	8-9-97
	321 lbs.	Marina Zhguleva	165 lbs.	Russia	6-20-97
	212 lbs.	Irina Krylova	106 lbs.	Russia	9-14-95

DEAD LIFT	Weight Lifted	Name	Body Weight	Nationality	Date of Lift
Men	895 lbs.	Lars Noren	276+ lbs.	Sweden	4-10-88
	744 lbs.	Dan Austin	165 lbs.	USA	7-30-94
	564 lbs.	E. S. Bhaskaran	115 lbs.	India	12-1-93
Junior Men	794 lbs.	Aarre Kapyla	205 lbs.	Finland	9-19-87
	740 lbs.	Sahroni	165 lbs.	INA	9-20-94
	535 lbs.	Dennis Thios	115 lbs.	INA	9-2-90
Women	579 lbs.	Katrina Robertson	198+ lbs.	Austria	6-21-97
	538 lbs.	Ruth Shafer	149 lbs.	USA	5-20-84
	364 lbs.	Nancy Belliveau	97 lbs.	USA	6-1-85
Junior Women	557 lbs.	Elena Suchoruk	165 lbs.	Ukraine	5-6-95
	419 lbs.	Oksana Belova	115 lbs.	Russia	6-27-96
	346 lbs.	Svetlana Tesleva	97 lbs.	Russia	12-6-96

The above records are a selection of weight class record holders. The top weight lifted in each class is the world record for that lift in that class. This information was compiled using data from the International Powerlifting Federation and the United States Weightlifting Federation.

STRENGTH TRAINING TALK

bodybuilding: A form of competition in which men and women pose to show judges their muscular development. The competitors are judged on the size, shape, definition of their muscles, which they develop through strength training.

calisthenics: Strength training exercises that use the body as resistance. Examples of calisthenic exercises are situps, pushups, crunches, side leg raises, dips, and pullups.

free weights: Barbells, dumbbells, and other equipment onto which weight plates can be loaded. A barbell is a long bar onto each end of which plates of varying weights can be loaded. Dumbbells are shorter bars that are usually used in pairs, one in each hand. Some dumbbells are simple bars onto which weights can be loaded, much like a barbell. Other dumbbells are weighted permanently with specific amounts of weight. For example, a set of dumbbells might consist of two 5-pound dumbbells, two 10-pound dumbbells, and two 15-pound dumbbells.

incline bench: A bench used with free weights that is set at an upward angle, typically about 45 degrees.

isotonic: A type of exercise in which muscles move and contract against resistance. Chinups and dumbbell curls are two of many examples of isotonic exercises. Isotonic exercises differ from isometric exercises, in which the muscles contract against resistance but do not move. Pushing against a stationary object is an example of isometric exercise.

metabolism: The chemical process by which the body utilizes food. The higher a person's metabolism, the more efficiently his or her body extracts and uses the nutrients consumed during a meal.

Olympic lifting: A form of competition in which participants attempt two lifts—the snatch and the clean and jerk. Each athlete gets three tries at each lift. For the snatch, the lifter must lift the barbell from the floor to overhead in one continuous movement. The clean and jerk consists of two motions—first the lifter raises the barbell to chest height and then raises it overhead as he or she stands. The best score for each lift is recorded, and the two scores are added for a total score.

power lifting: A form of competition in which the lifters get three tries each at the squat, the bench press, and the dead lift. For the squat, the lifter begins with the barbell across the back of the shoulders, then lowers the body by bending the knees until the thighs are parallel to the ground. For the bench press, the lifter lies on a bench facing up and lifts the barbell straight up from the chest. The lifter is in a standing position for the dead lift, grasping the barbell with one hand in an overhand grip and the other in an underhand grip. The barbell is lifted up from the ground as the lifter stands. The best score is taken for each lift. The three scores are added for a total score.

program: A long-term series of workout routines designed to work specific parts of the body on alternating days.

repetition: The completion of a single lift or exercise, such as one chinup, one bench press, or one squat.

resistance tools: Equipment for performing strength-training exercises without the use of weights. Rubber tubing is the most common resistance tool.

set: A series of repetitions of the same exercise. For example, a series of 10 consecutive Arnolds or 15 consecutive situps is a set. Normally, 1 to 4 sets of an exercise are done at a time.

weight machines: Machines equipped with weights for performing specific lifts. Nautilus, Universal, and Hydra-Gym weight machines use variable resistance, which

means they provide maximum resistance at the lifter's strongest position in the lift and ease up on resistance at the point of least strength. Cybex, Biodex, and Lido equipment perform in a similar way but also control the speed at which the weight is lifted.

workout routine: An organized grouping of sets that work several different parts of the body. For example, a workout routine could consist of 1 to 3 sets each of leg presses, squats, calf raises, situps, Arnolds, and bench presses.

FURTHER READING

Roberts, Scott, and Ben Weider. *Strength and Weight Training for Young Athletes.* Chicago: Contemporary Books, 1994.

Seidler, Todd L., and Debra L. Waters and Wendy L. Wilson. *Weight Training and Fitness for Health and Performance.* Dubuque, IA: Kendall/Hunt Publishing Company, 1990.

Smith, Tim. *Youth Strength Training.* North Palm Beach, FL: The Athletic Institute, 1988.

FOR MORE INFORMATION

Amateur Bodybuilding Association
Gold's Gym
1307 W 6th Street
Corona, CA 91720

National Strength and Conditioning
    Association
P. O. Box 81410
Lincoln, NE 68501

National Youth Sports Foundation
10 Meredith Circle
Needham, MA 02192

Strength of America, Inc.
P. O. Box 31447
Mesa, AZ 85275-1447

U. S. Powerlifting Federation, Inc.
P. O. Box 2170
Kilgore, TX 75663

U. S. Weightlifting Federation
One Olympic Plaza
Colorado Springs, CO 80909

INDEX